Muskets & Springfields

Wargaming the American Civil War 1861-1865

Nigel Emsen

Helion & Company Limited
Unit 8 Amherst Business Centre
Budbrooke Road
Warwick
CV34 5WE
England
Tel. 01926 499 619
Email: info@helion.co.uk
Website: www.helion.co.uk
Twitter: @helionbooks
Visit our blog http://blog.helion.co.uk/

Published by Helion & Company 2023
Designed and typeset by Nigel Emsen
Cover designed by Paul Hewitt, Battlefield Design (www.battlefield-design.co.uk)

Text © Nigel Emsen 2023
Illustrations © as individually credited
Colour artwork drawn by Giorgio Albertini © Helion & Company 2023
Maps and graphics created by Nigel Emsen © Helion & Company 2023

ISBN 978-1-804512-91-3

British Library Cataloguing-in-Publication Data.
A catalogue record for this book is available from the British Library.

For details of other military history titles published by Helion & Company Limited contact the above address or visit our website: http://www.helion.co.uk.

We always welcome receiving book proposals from prospective authors.

Contents

DEDICATION

To my lovely wife, best friend and soul mate Debbie,
for allowing 'just one more army' into the house.

Foreword

I have always been a huge fan of rule systems written by Nigel Emsen and *Muskets & Springfields* is no exception. Nigel is first and foremost a historian, with a fantastic mastery of his subject matter. Therefore, the games he designs are always well grounded in the history of the period he is writing about. Add this to his deep understanding of rule systems being both enjoyable and playable, the linking of these is often not a given in many sets of rules, and you have a combination which gives those playing his rules a first-class gaming experience. Further, Nigel's rules allow scalability, allowing different figure scales, figure numbers and table sizes to be used. They are therefore accessible to all gamers, widening the player base. For all those with a love of the history of, and gaming about the American Civil War, these rules are highly recommended.

Dr Simon Elliott
Honorary Research Fellow, University of Kent
Trustee, Council for British Archaeology
President, Society of Ancients.

ACKNOWLEDGMENTS

I would like to thank the following for all the play testing, input and ensuring the game design has stayed true to the original concepts.

Alan Curtis

Andy Pain

Simon Elliott

Stephen Stead

Introduction

Muskets & Springfields is designed for games representing big battles in the American Civil War. The rules are designed to use your current basing methods and are not miniature scale dependant. The game is set at the operational level. Players will adopt the role of the army commander with sub-command groups below him to represent corps or divisions. In the rules a corps or division will be made up of several infantry brigades, cavalry and your artillery batteries. If you wish you can include Native American Indian warbands as part of your games, although during the American Civil War their appearances in a pitched battle were very few and far between.

Game space

The game system uses grids as the unit of measurement. The game space is broken into square grids which represent 300 yards. The rules are focused on the operational level and so the specific tactical positioning of the unit, in yards from another unit, is deemed to be low level interaction that is not part of the scope of *Muskets & Springfields*. There are many commercial rulesets already available which provide this tactical level of play. Taking an average of the various drill guides of the period, a grid side is approximately equal to 600 men, deployed two ranks, regiments in line abreast. The average space needed of 24 inches per man has been used for this calculation. For a typical six-feet-by-four feet playing space, a ratio width by depth of one and a half by one is recommended, which provides a table divided into 12 by eight grid squares. This represents 3,600 yards by 2,400 yards in real ground scale. All units of measure for movement and ranges are presented as several grids. All measurements are taken relative to the grid side and orientation, not the unit base.

Game flow

Muskets & Springfields uses a 'bag pull' system using a deck of playing cards. The suit and colour of the card all have relevance in the game, as do the Joker cards. Confederates use the red suits and Union the black. The suit drawn determines the active player. The value of the card, for example the nine of Hearts, denotes the number of units in the player's army that can be activated, in this example, nine.

Activation is by corps. *Muskets & Springfields* allows a level of interruption for the non-active player. Also, each player has the option, once per game, to steal the draw.

These two approaches ensure if one player has a run of cards, the opponent still can respond. Also, aspects of the game such as shooting and melee are simultaneous. Jokers provide random narrative events to add to the game experience. The effects of the weather are also part of the Muskets & Springfields' game mechanics. Along with the overall game mechanics and the method by which morale is simulated, detailed later in these rules, this provides a nice 'fog of war' layer and a degree of 'controlled uncertainty'.

Force structure

The basic unit represented in the rules is the infantry brigade which is organised into corps and divisions. Attached to these formations are cavalry and artillery. These units are represented on the tabletop as a single base. The rules are designed to keep the movement, shooting and unit interactions as simple as possible. This allows the players to focus on the command decisions needed to manage multiple corps on the tabletop.

Morale

Morale loss is handled at the individual corps. Morale status and damage attrition markers are held on the individual unit base. In *Muskets & Springfields*, units have three levels of morale. These are not the usual '*average*', '*veteran*', '*elite*' grades often used, but instead, is in a format designed to reflect the actual state of mind of a unit on the day of battle. The unit morale levels are described as '*unknown*', '*nervous*' and '*steady*'. In a game, unless representing specific historical units, all bases start as '*unknown*'. The actual morale state is not known until the unit first takes damage. The player then rolls against the appropriate chart, dependant on the year the of the war in which the game is set. The chart provides a structure to be rolled against to see if the unit is '*nervous*' or '*steady*'. This threshold is also further divided into Confederate or Union. This is all encompassed under the 'fight or flight' rule.

When a unit fails a morale check, this is recorded against the parent corps. Once a corps reaches its breakpoint the whole formation is lost from the battlefield for the remainder of the game. The number of units in the corps will dictate the breakpoint for that corps.

Muskets & Springfields includes the traditional morale tests that wargamers are familiar with. The subtle difference is that a unit does not take a morale test till it has acquired three attrition hits. These are explained below. If a unit fails a morale test, then it is classed as broken and is removed from play. This keeps the game free flowing.

Attrition

Attrition is recorded at the unit level. This represents a loss of cohesion, battlefield casualties, a breakdown in fire discipline and ammunition running low. An individual unit can absorb five hits. On the sixth it is automatically destroyed. A unit must receive at least two hits in any one turn to test on the 'fight or flight' rule or to take a morale test. Attrition can be recorded with the unit using bespoke modelled tokens or a small D6. Once a unit starts to receive hits it can never recover below two hits in the in the game. With this limit we now have the concept of fresh troops. When a unit has received two hits this is the first level at which the number of hits begins to effect the efficiency of a unit.

Small arms and artillery representation

To facilitate a smooth flow of play and because Muskets & Springfields sits at the operational level, there is no separation between smoothbore and rifled small arms. Given the ground scale of one grid equals 300 yards, and often because of intervening terrain, potential targets at the longer ranges that rifles could achieve would be obscured. However, this distinction is included for artillery. The two distinctions are smoothbore artillery, that is more effective at close range, and rifled artillery, which is not disadvantaged when conducting counter-battery fire and shooting at longer ranges.

Vexillia: Martin Stephenson ©2023

Generals

There are two levels of command in the game. The army commander, which is you the player, and then at the next level down the corps or division commanders, which will be, as explained above, organised historically or just how you designed your army.

Generals are preferably modelled on a small disc. Generals have a command distance and the unit will need to be within this distance to be able to carry out any ordered action. Units do not have to finish a move within command distance. For example, a unit could advance if it is currently in command but it can end the move out of command distance. The army commander has no limit on command distance and is assumed to be all seeing, all reaching, on the tabletop.

Generals are by default, classed at a competent level for the period. Generals can also be better than this, for example the rules allow for exceptional generals, who can be army or corps commanders. An example might be Hancock. Exceptional generals add an extra command token into the pool. At the other end of the scale, we have generals of questionable quality. These are generals with no experience and more than likely will be a political appointee, Sickles for example. Questionable quality generals cause a command token to be removed from the pool.

Vexillia: Martin Stephenson ©2023

Orders

In Muskets & Springfields, we also include the concept of orders. These are an optional aspect of the rules. There are three types of orders; defend, probe and attack. Orders are applied at corps level. Orders can only be changed by the army commander and by expending a command token. A corps needs to be activated to have its orders changed.

The defend order means you are only allowed to move up to a third of your deployed bases out of your deployment zone and sector. However, with defend orders, you can exchange infantry brigades for fortifications. When you trade these infantry brigades this will bring down your corps breakpoint. If you are playing a historical scenario and then set up the troops and any defences according to their historical deployment.

The second type of order is probe. This means you must move at least a quarter and up to a third of your units, which must advance to within two squares of the enemy and start to engage. These units may move between sectors whereas with defend orders you must remain in your sector.

The third type of order is attack. Here you must move at least three-quarters of the corps in question to within two grid squares of the enemy and start to engage, and a third of these units must use their maximum movement rate to try and get within two squares. This rule is specifically designed to stop players from giving attack orders and dithering and effectively doing something between probe and defend.

Orders are kept hidden from your opponent. You can write them on a piece of paper and keep them safe or make little tokens and put them face down behind the general.

Vexillia: Martin Stephenson ©2023

Scales

This chapter explains the representaion of units, suggested basing and game space.

Representation

The rules are designed for the more common six-feet-by-four feet game table, which represents in the case of these rules the operational area for several corps or divisions.

Basing

These rules use a ratio system of a base representing several men or guns. These are detailed in the table below (basing does not matter as the grid system is used on the tabletop):

Base type	Representation	Width relative to grid
Artillery Gun line	A battery deployed in firing line across the frontage	1
Infantry	Infantry brigade	
Infantry with Zouaves	Infantry brigade with Zouaves intergrated	
Mounted cavalry	Regiment of approximately 300 mounted troopers.	
Dismounted Cavalry	Dismounted troopers with horse holders	0.5
Native American warbands	Mixed foot and mounted warriors	
Sharpshooters	50+ sharpshooters dispersed in skirmish order.	
Skirmisher deployed markers	A skirmish line has been deployed forward from the main body.	Disc

Base depth

As minimal as possible to fit in with the ground scale, but this is not critical to the game.

Time elapsed

Once the card deck has been used this is deemed to signal the end of a full day's combat, from dawn to dusk or dusk to dawn.

Unit of measurement

The unit of measurement used for ranges and movement is one grid square. This allows players quite a bit of flexibility in how they use their current collection. All the charts and rules show distances in grid squares. Distance one is the next grid. However, grids that are diagonal to the starting grid count as one and a half grid squares in distance.

Game space

The rules can be played on any size board space. Typically, this will be a six-by-four-foot table. However, players can increase or decrease the table size depending on the scale and size of forces being used.

From the author's 20mm Airfix collection

Ground scale

The ground scale is one grid represents a square area 300 yards by 300 yards.

Grids

The tabletop should be broken down into a grid of squares. It is recommended to just spot the corners of the grid squares on a game matt. This avoids the need to draw lines across the playing surface. Apart from aiding remote internet play, grids provide a simplified way for measuring distances and the positioning of bases.

Model Scale	Recommended grid size	Game space ratio (1.5 × 1)	Ground scale on six-by-four
40mm+	Twelve inches	Six grids × four grids	1,800 yards × 1,200 yards
25mm–28mm	Eight inches	Nine grids × six grids	2,700 yards × 1,800 yards
10mm to 20mm	Six inches	Twelve grids × eight grids	3,600 yards × 2,400 yards
2mm to 6mm	Four inches	Eighteen grids × twelve grids	5,400 yards × 3,600 yards

Note: The above grid sizes are recommendations, and the players can adopt a size that matches the game size they would like to represent using their current models and basing. The rules rely on an agnostic approach to base widths as the actual size of the physical base is not critical, as long as it fits within the grid width.

Occupation limits

Grids can only be occupied by two bases from any single army.

1. Only one artillery base can count as being unlimbered/deployed into a firing line in a single grid, even if orientated against a different grid side
2. General, sharpshooter bases and skirmisher markers are excluded from this restriction
3. Only one sharpshooter base can finish the end of their movement in a grid

Base orientation within a grid

Base orientation within a grid is important.

1. The orientation defines the front edge of the base

2. Bases cannot be orientated diagonally

3. They must be either parallel with a long side edge or a short side edge of the game space

4. Bases that are deployed behind an infantry, dismounted or mounted cavalry base on the edge of the grid square and in the same orientation are blocked for line of sight

Interpenetration of bases through a grid

A base can move through a grid occupied only by friendly bases. If a base's movement does not exceed one grid square, then two bases can swap one base over. A swapped base is considered as having completed all prompted actions for this turn.

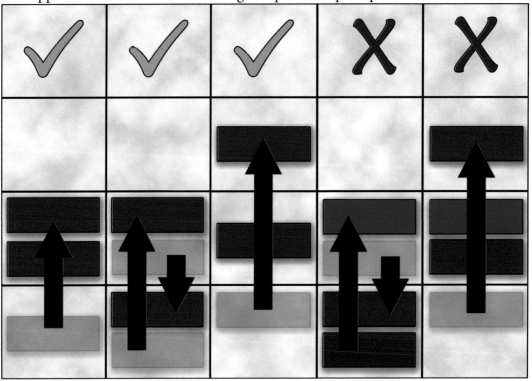

Sectors

The game space needs to be split into three sectors. These are each one-third of the overall width in grids by the full depth of the game space. These three sectors are named as follows and are relative to the individual players perspective:

1. Left flank sector

2. Centre sector

3. Right flank sector

These sectors are shown below from the players' perspective:

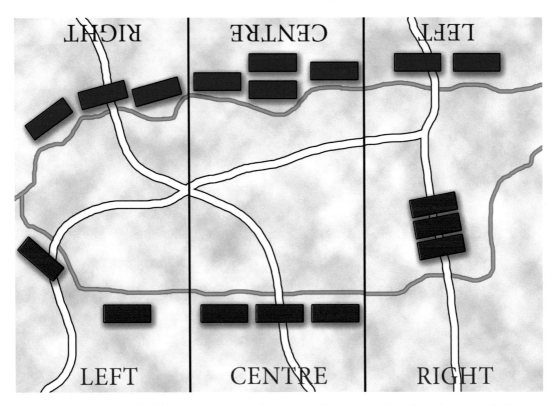

Sectors are specifically important to the game objectives that the players roll for during the game setup phase. Players play from one long edge to the other. Bases can arrive on any edge but can only leave via a player's long edge.

Army structure

A game is aimed at the multi-corps level with a distinct focus on command and control.

Corps & division command formations

At certain times during the war a Confederate corps could be twice the size of a Union one. The number of bases needed can be calculated from the scales above. Artillery and sharpshooters are not included in the number of bases detailed in the table below. This is because their attachment varied through the war for individual corps and divisions. To facilitate a simple way of representing the different command formations sizes we have three distinct levels. These are detailed in the table below:

Command Formation	Typical representation	Bases	Breakpoint
Small	1,800 men	3	Four morale hits
Medium	1,900–4,800 men	4–8	Six morale hits
Large	4,900+ men	9+	Eight morale hits

The players will each represent the most senior commander in their respective armies, so if a single large corps is being fielded, then the player would be the corps commander.

1. If several corps or attached independent reinforced bases are being fielded, then the player would represent the army commander

2. Only one sub-level from the army commander is represented in a game. This is the level immediately down from the army commander and only as far as base level

3. An army must include at least three (corps) command formations

4. Unless playing a historical scenario, an army must have an odd number of corps in total

5. Confederate armies must include at least one large corps

Base types

Units can be made up of several smaller bases using an existing collection to create the required frontage or a single vignette base. The author has adopted a single square base using the vignette approach, largely for appearance and ease of play. The different types of bases are defined below.

Artillery

An artillery base represents 24 guns with supporting caissons. When unlimbered, they always count as in open order for line of sight and shooting.

1. Shooting from artillery ignores cover adjustments except where these are blocking line of sight
2. Shooting from artillery can ignore all open order bases in any grid in line of sight
3. Gun models and crew are based separately. During the game, the crew can be driven off, leaving the guns available for capture

An artillery battery is further broken down into the following two types. All artillery in the game should fit into one of the two categories detailed below. Any mortars within a battery are assumed to be absorbed into one of the two types defined below:

No distinction is made between foot and horse batteries.

Deployment and unlimbering restriction:

Only one artillery battery can unlimber and deploy into a firing line in a single grid square.

Smoothbore artillery:

This category covers all smoothbore 6pdr and 12pdr guns.

Rifled artillery:

This represents all artillery that are rifled.

MUSKETS & SPRINGFIELDS

Capturing enemy guns

When the position of an artillery battery is in contact with any base except a general base and additionally the gun crew base is not present, the cannon constituting the battery are considered captured. There are two immediate options open to the capturing player:

1. Spike the guns. This option must be taken unless the guns count as captured. When spiked, both the guns and crew are immediately removed from play for the remainder of the game causing a morale hit
2. Capture. Only an infantry base may elect to capture the guns
    I. When an artillery base is captured for the first time in the game, it causes a morale hit on the army
    II. From the next player's turn, the infantry base may fire the artillery if the capturing infantry base remains to its front, long edge base to long edge base, and in contact with the battery
    III. When electing to fire captured artillery, the infantry base can shoot but uses the reduced dice as if skirmishers are deployed
    IV. The captured artillery cannot be moved or turned in any way
    V. If the infantry base that captured the artillery battery is no longer in contact with the artillery base, then the artillery base immediately counts as spiked and is removed from the game

Cavalry

A cavalry base represents a unit. Cavalry bases can dismount and operate as infantry if required. A mounted cavalry base is never counted out of command distance from their commanding general.

Cavalry raider rule (optional)

Cavalry that will remain mounted for the whole game may apply the following rules:

1. After rolling for objectives, the players may elect to place any cavalry bases off-board to arrive as raiders
2. The players must document and keep hidden from their opponents on which board zone and board edge they will arrive
3. A mounted cavalry base may arrive via the opponent's long edge if the player wishes.
4. A cavalry base must be allocated to a general other than the army commander at deployment
5. The mounted cavalry base arrives on a draw of an Ace, King, Queen or Jack of the player's suit
6. The base cannot arrive on the first turn and must wait for the next appropriate card to be drawn
7. The command group which a mounted cavalry base is part of must be also one that is activated on that draw if possible
8. The base must be placed on the board at the start of that turn
9. A cavalry base cannot be blocked from entering the board
10. If the cavalry base is blocked by enemy bases from arriving, then those blocking bases must make the minimum amount of movement backwards so that they are in an adjacent grid square from the cavalry base. If this is not possible then the blocking base is moved the minimum number of grid squares to be legally placed in a grid
11. The cavalry bases are placed with their long rear edge fully aligned and in contact with the board edge they arrived on
12. A cavalry base that is first placed on the board cannot complete any other actions until their owning next players turn
13. A dismounted cavalry base must meet the command distance rules
14. A command group with cavalry raiders can only use attack orders
15. A player must declare at the end of deployment if the army contains cavalry raiders which have been sent off-board

Dismounted cavalry

Cavalry may dismount and form into a firing line with horse holders. When dismounted they may deploy a skirmish line forward. Dismounted cavalry bases are affected by command distance.

Infantry bases

An infantry base represents several regiments as a brigade of up to 600 men. Infantry bases may deploy a skirmish line.

Vexillia: Martin Stephenson ©2023

Native American warbands (optional)

These bases represent a warband of Native Americans who can be all mounted, all dismounted or a mixture of mounted and dismounted. The base moves at a set distance, regardless of the mix of foot and mounted.

It should be noted that Native Americans were actually rarely present in Civil War battles but have been included to provide an element of something different and interesting. Where they were present in small numbers.

Sharpshooters

This represents a small detachment in skirmish order that snipes at enemy formations. These men would be proficient shooters and often but not always, armed with one of the more advanced rifles of the period. A maximum of one base per corps is permitted and only one may finish movement in a grid.

Skirmishers

Infantry bases and dismounted cavalry may throw forward a skirmish line. This is represented by a single base of one or more models.

1. A skirmish line, when deployed, extends the shooting range, but the parent base shoots at a reduced rate
2. A skirmish line can only be deployed to the front of the parent base
3. If enemy infantry, Native American warbands or cavalry (mounted or dismounted) are at one grid distance to the parent base front, after completing movement, the skirmish line is automatically forced to return to the parent base and the marker is removed from the tabletop
4. The defender can deploy skirmishers at the deployment stage representing forward pickets. The attacker must do so during normal gameplay

Zouaves infantry bases

These are represented in an infantry brigade in which the majority of the regiments are Zouaves, who wore flamboyant uniforms at the start of the war. Over time the Zouaves generally adopted the regular uniform. For game context and presence, Zouaves have advantages in melee but can be an easier target for shooting.

Zouave rule (optional)

By the start of 1863 these units had started to convert to the regular uniform of the army, although even towards the end of the war some regiments had not completed this conversion. There is an optional rule for shooting included if players wish to bring this concept into the game. Shooters gain a plus to hit.

Generals

These represent all generals with their staff, and they are mounted on a circular base. A general can move during the game. Generals' bases cannot be targeted directly in the game but are at risk from combat going on in their presence.

Command distance

Generals have a command range which limits the area of influence. These are detailed in the table below:

General	Command distance in grid squares
Army commander	No limit
Other generals	3

A base needs to be in command distance to be able to initiate any action but does not have to end in command distance at the end of an action. Permitted actions are detailed in the actions chapter later in these rules.

Command tokens

Command tokens provide a method by which a player has a finite number of chances to influence the flow of the battle. Either player can interrupt the play sequence.

At the start of the game each player receives six command tokens, held with the army commander. The army commander starts game with six tokens, but this can be adjusted by the optional 'Exceptional and questionable general' rule below:

Exceptional army commander (optional rule)

Where the army or a corps is led by an exceptional general this provides an extra command token. Add one token to the total available at the start of the game.

Questionable army commander (optional rule)

Where the army is led by a general of questionable abilities, then this will cause a reduction in the available command tokens. Remove one token from the total available at the start of the game.

Army commander (Commander-in-Chief)

The army commander is represented by a base, ideally a circular one, although this is not critical.

An army commander can complete the following command actions and does not need to be activated or the owning player to be the active player:

Cost	Action
One token	Reform one corps attrition if not the active player.
	Force a success on 1D10.
	Add 1D10 to any throw that requires D10s.
	Change any corps orders if the active player.
Free	Move once per turn as mounted cavalry if the active player.
	If present in the same grid allow 1D10 to be re-rolled per throw for any base in the army, that has not been re-rolled.
	Grabbing battlefield initiative

Grabbing battlefield initiative

Once per game the army commander can attempt to grab the initiative and counts as an Ace card in the player's suit. This overrules the card drawn.
1. This option cannot be claimed on the first draw
2. It can only be claimed if after the turn card has been drawn and the player is not the active player
3. The opposing player cannot counter-claim battlefield initiative

Other generals

Generals which are not the army commander are represented by a circular base, although this is not critical. They move as mounted cavalry.

A general can complete the following command actions:

Cost	Action (see command actions section)
Free	Move once per turn as mounted cavalry when part of an activated corps.
	If present in the same grid allow 1D10 to be re-rolled per throw for a base in their command, that has not been re-rolled.

Risk to generals

When generals are close to the action there is a risk they can be incapacitated. If a general is in the same grid that receives four attrition hits in total for a single turn, then a risk to general test must be completed.

Risk to generals method

1. The opposing player rolls 1D6 to for each general in the grid
2. On a score of a natural six a general has been disabled/killed

When an army commander is disabled/killed:

1. The base is temporary removed from play
2. No benefit can be drawn from the army commander until the next player's turn
3. No command tokens can be played until the next player's turn
4. All friendly bases in the same grid as the general who was killed take one attrition hit
5. A new general is appointed at the start of the player's next draw of the cards and is placed in a grid of the owning player's choice, and which also has a corps general already present

When other generals are disabled/killed

The following effects are applied:

1. The base is temporary removed from play
2. That corps takes a morale hit
3. No benefit can be drawn from the corps commander until the next player's turn
4. A new general is appointed at the start of the player's next turn and is placed in a grid with bases from that corps
5. If no bases remain on the table for that corps, then the general does not return and any off-board cavalry raiders are lost for the remainder of the game

Morale

All bases have different levels of resilience to the effects of battle. This is commonly known as morale. Morale is broken down into three basic levels and these are detailed below.

Nervous

These are inexperienced units that are uneasy about the forthcoming battle or veteran bases where their motivation on the day is in question.

Steady

These units have experience of battle and can be relied upon in most situations to perform satisfactorily. They could be well trained and led, have a high proportion of veterans within the ranks or be more resilient than the balance of the remainder of the army. Ignore the first attrition hit received in a turn whether active or not.

Unknown

Where a unit's willingness is not known until after first contact with the enemy, these bases are always classed as unknown. This uncertainty is reflected in varying outcomes in the game. All bases start the game as Unknown. On receiving a total of two attrition hits in a single turn, immediately apply the *Flight or Fight rule* to the affected base before proceeding further.

The Fight or Flight rule

The rule is triggered when a base receives two attrition hits and is classed as unknown. Players can use the optional year table below or use a score of 5+ on a D6 for the base to count as steady. Roll 1D6 and consult the table below. A successful roll means the base is steady otherwise counts as nervous. Note 1863 represents the period until the end of day three of the Battle of Gettysburg. 1863/Post covers the rest of the year in the aftermath of the Confederate defeat.

1. If the result is nervous, the base receives two hits
2. If the result is steady, the base receives one hit

Year Table (Optional)

Army	1861	1862	1863	1863/Post	1864	1865
CSA	3	3	4	5	5	5
Union	5	4	4	3	4	3

Morale tests

During the game there will be situations that will require a morale test to be taken. The situations are defined below:

1. After receiving attrition hits in a single turn and the base has greater than two attrition hits applied
2. Check to charge or receive a charge. A morale check resulting in a failure to charge does not inflict a morale hit on the testing base's corps

Method

1. Consult the tables below to obtain the required score
2. Throw 1D10 and check against the outcomes table below

Situation by base	Adjust
If Zouaves or a Native American war party testing to charge or be charged	Auto pass
Base	5
Has other steady bases in same grid	−1
If counting rear supported	
For a general in line of command (maximum of one) in the same grid	
For each attrition hit over two	+1
If charging from cover into the open/from open into cover	
If the required score is more than 10, then it is an automatic failure by a score of one, and command tokens cannot be applied to affect this result.	

Outcomes

After throwing the D10, note the difference thrown against the required score. Consult the table below:

Effect (Not chargers)	Result
Pass, remove one morale hit from the unit's corps	Natural 10
Pass, continue	equal/greater than 0
Fail, base is immediately destroyed	Less than 0
Effect (Chargers)	**Result**
Fail, does not charge and no other effect is applied	<0

From the author's 20mm Airfix collection

Recording damage

Losses are measured and recorded at two levels. Firstly, the overall morale of a specific corps and secondly at the unit level with attrition. These differences are detailed below.

Attrition hits

During battle a unit will experience the ebb and flow of battle, the effects of attrition and fighting ability. This is represented in the game by attrition hits. When a base receives six attrition hits it is destroyed and removed from play. This represents the complete psychological breakdown in the unit's ranks as well as other elements such as actual casualties and expenditure of resources.

1. At the end of the current turn, the active player can reduce attrition hits from any activated corps. See *Reducing attrition hits* below
2. The non-active player may elect to reduce attrition hits See *Reducing attrition hits* below
3. This is done before the next card is drawn from the deck

Reducing attrition hits

When reducing attrition hits on a base the following limits apply:
1. Any base in an activated corps can reduce by one attrition hit
2. The non-active player may elect to expend one command token for this turn, to reduce all bases by one attrition hit
3. No base, once it has hits applied to it, can be reduce these losses below two but may carry a single hit until it reaches two or more hits for the first time during the game

Destroyed bases

1. When a base is broken immediately when they reach six attrition hits
2. When a base fails a morale test other than to charge
3. When a base is destroyed their corps takes one morale hit

Morale hits

In *Muskets & Springfields*, morale is managed at the command formation level. This is usually a corps. See the command formation table above for the morale break point. When the amount of morale damage reaches the number specified, then the command formation immediately breaks. When a command formation breaks it cannot be recovered in the game.

When units fail morale tests

When this happens and is not the result of testing to charge, they count as broken and are out of action for the rest of the game.

1. The base is immediately removed from play
2. Their corps takes a morale hit
3. If the corps has reached the break point limit, the corps counts as a command formation break

When a command formation breaks:

1. All bases in the command formation count as broken and will count as destroyed
2. All bases from that corps removed from the board expect the artillery gun base. Artillery gun bases are left in situ can be captured by the enemy or recaptured
3. The general of the broken command formation is immediately removed from play
4. Enemy bases, except unlimbered artillery, in an adjacent grid may optionally advance and occupy the grid if the grid is completely cleared of enemy bases

Orders (optional)

During the game setup phase after deployment, all corps must be given one of the three order types detailed below.

During the game these initial orders can be changed by the army commander, by using an action. Orders are kept hidden from the opponent; players can record them separately or have then on tokens face down with the general's base.

Order	Game effects
Defend	Only up to one third of deployed bases can leave the deployment zone and sector initially placed into.
	May trade one infantry base for one fortification. If this is done check the corps size and adjust break point.
Probe	One quarter to one third of bases deployed must advance until two squares or less from the enemy and engage.
	May move into another sector.
Attack	Three-quarters or more of deployed bases must advance until two squares from the enemy and engage. Up to a third of bases deployed must be two squares or less from the enemy or attempt to achieve this using the greatest movement distance available, if they are activated.

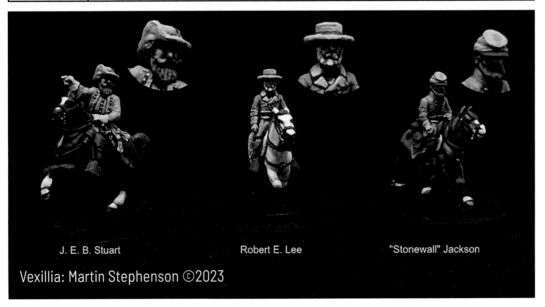

J. E. B. Stuart   Robert E. Lee   "Stonewall" Jackson

Vexillia: Martin Stephenson ©2023

Actions

Depending on the available action points a base can complete the following:

1. A single base cannot perform more than two actions in any given turn
2. Actions are broken down into base and command actions
3. Command actions are detailed in the command tokens section above
4. The number of active corps depends on the type of card drawn

Prompted base actions

The following actions can only be completed by an active base. The base must start within command distance of their corps commander. However, the base does not have to finish within command distance.

Charges

This is where the base charges straight ahead into a grid occupied by an enemy base.

1. The charge must be directly into the target grid, on the same grid side and with the same orientation as the chargers.
2. A charging base is deemed be charging all enemy bases in the target grid.
3. The active player may select any or all bases that are eligible to charge from a given grid.
4. A charge declaration can only include active bases from an active corps.
5. A base can only charge/attempt to charge once per turn.
6. A base can be charged any number of times by different bases and can conduct defensive fire each time.

The following are bases which are eligible to charge

1. Any base except artillery and sharpshooters can charge any enemy base. Artillery and sharpshooters can never charge
2. Skirmishers can never be charged directly. The charge must be able to reach the parent base. If the parent base is charged, they will return automatically to the parent base
3. Corps generals not in the same grid as friendly bases will move directly away from the direction of the charge into the next adjacent grid, or the next available grid towards the player's long edge that is not occupied by any enemy bases
4. All bases test to charge and if successful the target base tests for being charged unless they are eligible to scoot, or to shoot and scoot
5. Artillery crew must attempt to shoot and scoot if a friendly infantry base is in the same grid or else may elect to shoot and scoot, or scoot, or stand. Artillery only takes a morale test for being charged if they elect to stand
6. Sharpshooters must either attempt to shoot and scoot or scoot and do not take a morale test for being charged
7. Sharpshooters can never charge but can be charged
8. Dismounted cavalry may attempt to scoot. They cannot shoot and scoot

How to conduct a charge

1. Player declares all bases that are charging, the charge route and target grid. The number of declared charging bases cannot exceed the occupation limits of any given grid square. The move is measured and fully explained to the opponent before any morale tests are taken. This ensures a player cannot declare extra bases in case any fail to charge
2. Every charging base in the grid takes a morale test to charge.
3. If they fail, then no further action is allowed from that base. A failure to charge does not cause a morale hit
4. Move the charging bases that passed their morale test into the target grid, ensuring that the occupation limits are not exceeded by the chargers. Occupation limits apply separately to each player
5. All bases in the target grid now take a morale test for being charged and resolve any outcomes
6. Any remaining charged bases on a grid edge may now conduct defensive fire.
7. Position any bases that can claim a flank or rear charge so that they are easily identifiable for the melee
8. The melee is resolve at the end of the turn

Movement

Bases in the same grid as enemy bases cannot move except to:

1. Turn to face an enemy base in contact to its flank
2. Disengage one grid square from the current one and must move closer to the player's long edge
3. Disengaging bases may not interpenetrate through to another grid other than the adjacent grid
4. To move into front base-to-base contact with an enemy base already in the same grid

Disengage from a melee

Any base that has resolved the current turn of melee can elect to move one square directly into a grid not occupied by enemy bases and must be towards the player's long table edge. If the base disengages it takes one attrition hit prior to the physical movement.

Change direction

This is where the base changes facing in a grid. It must finish parallel to a table edge.

Deploy/recall skirmishers

This is where a base can deploy or recall already deployed skirmishers. The parent base can remain static or be part of movement. The skirmisher marker is placed in front of the base. This cannot be done as part of a shooting action.

Limber/unlimber artillery

An artillery base can be limbered or unlimbered. To be able to move, except to turn 90 or 180 degrees with no other movement, it must be limbered. To be able to shoot in any circumstances, the artillery must be unlimbered. In either situation the artillery must have the crew base with the gun model base to complete any action during the turn.

Move

The base moves directly ahead according to the Charge & Movement chart. A base may turn at the start or end of a move. A base can only turn once per action.

Charge and movement distances

The following table shows the charge and movement distances. The distances are also used for any movement involving a scoot action.

Base	Distance
Any moving through any sight-blocking cover (expect sharpshooters) Total movement allowed in the current turn. Ignore if fully on road during the turn	1
Infantry base	
Dismounted cavalry	
Charge distance (all)	
Shoot and scoot	
Sharpshooters	2
Mounted cavalry	
Limbered artillery	
Scoot only	
Movement entirely on road	+1 to above

Shooting

Due to the overall scale of the game, traditional close-and-long-range mechanics are not used. It is assumed the open space between bases there will be a level of small unit interaction going on.

1. Artillery must have crew or the capturing infantry base in contact with the guns to be able to shoot
2. A single base can only shoot at another single base
3. The shooting dice from a single shooting base cannot be split onto different target bases
4. Only one base can shoot from a grid side. The exception is that one sharpshooter base can also shoot in addition to any other bases shooting from a grid side
5. Sharpshooters can be shot through by friendly or enemy units
6. Skirmishers can be shot through by enemy units
7. If unlimbered artillery that is shot or will be shot through by friendly units it can not shoot as a prompted action in the current turn

Shooting arcs

1. Bases can only shoot to their front and 45 degrees to either side of straight ahead
2. Unlimbered artillery and sharpshooters are assumed to be forward of other types of bases, irrespective of their physical location along the grid edge. They do not block line of sight for shooting

Target priority

Target priorities are defined as follows. Sharpshooters or skirmishers can be ignored for shooting priority and do not take any damage if ignored.

Base Type	Range <=1	Range >1
Artillery	Most direct to front.	Most direct to front and nearest, or else, nearest in arc.
Sharpshooters	Most direct to front and nearest.	
All others	Most direct to front and nearest, or else, nearest in arc.	
Responsive	Must return fire to the shooters and only the shooters. This overrules the above.	

Conducting a shooting action

To conduct a shooting action, complete the following steps (when the active player's base shoots, the non-active player simultaneously returns fire):

1. Check range and arc
2. Calculate shooting chance
3. Calculate number of shooting dice
4. Throw the dice
5. Apply hits
6. Resolve outcomes

Ranges

The following tables show the ranges for shooting. In these rules, which are army-level/operational rules, no distinction has been made between the different types of small arms.

Small arms	Range in grids	Artillery	Range in grids
All small arms	1	Smoothbore	5
If skirmishers are deployed	2	Rifled	6
Any sharpshooters			

To hit chance

The following table calculates the hit chance needed to be thrown on the shooting dice:

Condition	Adjustment
Base factor for all shooting	5
All	
If shooting and scooting	+1
Target is sharpshooters or deployed artillery	
Shooters (small arms)	
If target in cover	+1
Has >1 hits currently applied	
If sharpshooters and range to target is 1	−1
If sharpshooters shooting at artillery	
Has not or will not move this turn	
Steady shooting at *nervous*	
Shooters (smoothbore artillery)	
Target range is >1	+2
Target range is 1	−1
Shooters (rifled artillery)	
Target range is >1	+1
Rifled artillery shooting at artillery >1	−1

Shooting dice

The number of shooting dice per base is defined in the following table:

Small arms	Dice
Infantry base	4D10
Infantry base with skirmishers deployed	3D10
Dismounted cavalry base	3D10
Dismounted cavalry base with skirmishers deployed	2D10
If target is enfiladed and target not sharpshooters	Auto 1 hit + dice thrown result(s)
If target is in fortifications	Re-roll hits
Sharpshooters	**Dice**
Sharpshooters (all situations)	1D10
Artillery	**Dice**
Target at range of one (smoothbore)	5D10
Target at range of one (rifled)	4D10
Target at range of over one	2D10
Target at range of six	1D10
If target is enfiladed and target not sharpshooters	Auto 1 hit + dice thrown result(s)

Outcomes

Consult the table below and resolve any effects:

Effect	Outcome
Each success per D10 (Except a natural 10)	One attrition hit
Small arms at range one throwing a natural 10. Suppressing fire	Two attrition hits
Artillery only shooting at more than one grid: (bounce through). On a natural 1D10, for each base except skirmisher markers, sharpshooters or a general	Throw 1D10 per unit using same value and apply as above
Hits applied and if target base has more than two attrition hits	Morale test

Free base actions

The following actions do not cost any action points and the base does not need to be in command distance to complete.

Conduct melee

At the end of the moving phase resolve all melees for units in contact with the enemy. The order of the melees is dictated by the active player.

Return fire as the non-phasing player

This is where the target base of the non-active player which is being shot at and it must return fire at the enemy shooting at them.

1. This return fire is completed simultaneously
2. If the target base has had to move due to an outcome in the current turn, then this movement is factored in. This applies in response to a shooting or charge action
3. When charging, in order to be able to return fire the charged base must have passed its morale test to receive the charge and chargers must have passed their test to charge

Turn to face enemy passing in adjacent grid

When an enemy base moves into an adjacent grid to the flank or rear, the non-active player may turn to face one base if the following conditions are met:

1. The base being turned to face is not artillery
2. The base is not facing another enemy base in an adjacent grid
3. No enemy bases are in the same grid square as the grid square in which the non-active player is intending to turn a base
4. The base must start the turn parallel with a table edge and finish parallel to a table edge

Reactive base actions

The following actions are reactive for the non-phasing player. Although free, they do carry a risk of a 1D6 dice roll which needs to be passed to complete the action. A roll of one is an automatic failure and no part of the action being attempted is possible. These actions replace the morale test for being charged.

Scoot only

Score needed to pass: 2+ on 1D6.

This is where sharpshooters scoot away from chargers, artillery crew can scoot away to a friendly infantry base, and any cavalry charged by infantry or Native American warband. Failure to scoot means the charged base does not move, except to face away from the charge and counts as caught evaders.

Shoot and scoot

Score needed to pass: 4+ on 1D6.

This is the same as scoot only, except a quick volley is fired before making the scoot move. If the shoot and scoot test is failed, then the action is converted into a successful *scoot only* response.

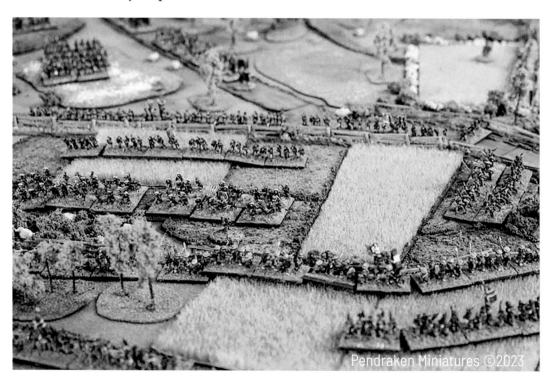

Command actions

The following actions can only be completed by a general and only apply to bases under a general's chain of command. To be able to complete a command action, action points or command tokens need to be available for that general.

Where a command action influences a specific base in any way then that base must be in command distance to gain any benefit. Command actions between two generals are assumed to be always in command distance. Generals move as if mounted cavalry, with the exception that they are not affected by cover or terrain in any way when moving. The general can move once per turn but must be activated.

Army commander actions

The following can only be actioned by the army commander:

- Reform one corps' attrition hits (costing one command token if not activated)
- Any bases, including those classed as nervous in a chosen corps, can remove one attrition hit. All bases can never have less than two attrition hits in any circumstances, i.e. once it has reached two attrition hits these can never be reduced further
- Change corps orders (free and must be activated)
- Can change the orders of any corps in the army. The new orders are effective from the next turn draw for the player. This delay simulates the dissemination of the orders down through division and unit commanders
- Expend one command token to add 1D10 to a roll (costing one command token)
- Any player may exchange one command token for 1D10 to add to a roll being made by a base in that corps. A maximum of 1D10 can be added to a single roll. This action must be declared before any dice are thrown
- Expend one command token to force a success on 1D10 (for the cost of one command token)
- Any player may exchange one command token to force a success on 1D10 roll. Only 1D10 can be influenced in any single roll. This action must be declared before any dice are thrown

Melee

Any bases in a grid square with an enemy base present must engage in a melee. An individual melee includes all the bases in the grid and is calculated as a single melee. All melees are conducted simultaneously at the end of each turn. These include resolving any charges in the current turn.

How to conduct melee

The following steps describe how to conduct a melee. A base can only fight another single base. A base cannot split the dice between different target dice:

1. Any grid with bases with an occupancy size of less than two must engage in melee if opposing bases are present in the same grid
2. Bases can only enter a grid already occupied solely by an enemy base using a charge action
3. Bases must be positioned so that they are parallel with a table edge
4. All bases in a grid are engaged in melee whether in base-to-base contact or not
5. The active player may move a base already in the grid that is not in front-edge contact to be in front-edge contact with an enemy base that does not have a base already in front-edge contact, or parallel behind a friendly base that is in front-edge contact with an enemy base
6. The non-active player then completes the steps in 5 above
7. Alternate steps 5 to 6 until all eligible bases are allocated
8. See diagram below with examples of different situations that can arise
9. Resolve each pairing of bases simultaneously until all melees in a grid have been completed. Repeat for all grids
10. Calculate the chance to hit using the following table for each base

Situation	Adjust
Base	5
Zouaves and Native American warbands	−2
Steady vs nervous	−1
Fighting enemy in cover/obstacle	+1
Or, fighting enemy in fortifications	+2
Mounted cavalry vs infantry base	Re-roll hits
First round charging into a flank	Re-roll misses

11. For each base, calculate the number of dice to be thrown looking for the chance to hit defined above

Base type	Dice
Infantry base	6D10
Cavalry (dismounted) or Zouaves	4D10
Native Indian war party in cover	4D10
Native Indian war party not in cover	2D10
Cavalry (mounted)	
Artillery crew	2D10
Sharpshooters	1D10
For each two attrition hits	−1D10
A base will always get to throw 1D10.	

12. Throw the dice for each individual base combat and note the number of successes
13. If a base is being attacked by several bases, then the owning player must decide which of the attacking bases is the target. This means the other attacking bases have a free throw
14. Decide the winner. This is the base that has thrown more than the enemy base
15. If the winner is a Native American war party, then add one to the total hits scored
16. The winner takes the difference in the two sets of dice scores, less one of this value. This means the winner could take zero hits
17. The loser takes the number of hits thrown by the opponent
18. Apply the hits as attrition hits to the appropriate bases
19. The main base that is engaged takes the total hits, then any surplus hits are applied to the supporting bases in the grid
20. Repeat for all bases in the current grid
21. Any winner that receives more than one attrition hit after all melee has been resolved for the current grid must take a morale test. Apply the outcome immediately
22. The loser always takes a morale test. Apply the outcome immediately
23. If it is a draw then both bases take the number of hits scored but do not take a morale test unless nervous troops vs steady, in which case the nervous base takes a morale test

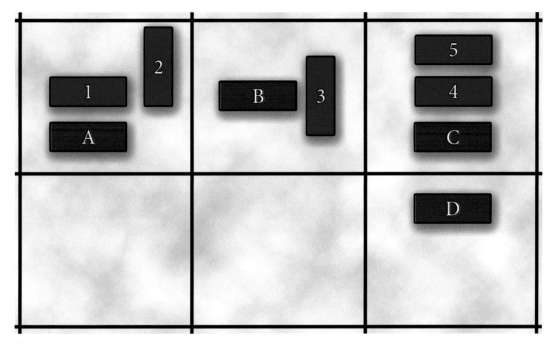

Examples

1. Bases A & base 2 engage each other in melee. Base 1 cannot be included in melee of base A & 2 because base 1 is not parallel with base 2
2. Base B & base 3 engage each other in melee
3. Base C & base 4 engage each other in melee. Base 5 is included as it is in the same grid and parallel with the supporting base. Base D cannot support base C because they are not in the same grid unless it has charged in and does not exceed stacking limits

Pendraken Miniatures ©2023

Rear support

This section details when rear support can be claimed. Rear support improves a base's chance of passing a morale test. To claim rear support the following conditions must be met:

- Only infantry and cavalry bases in the same grid can provide rear support
- Infantry and dismounted cavalry provide rear support each other
- Cavalry and dismounted cavalry provide rear support to each other
- Artillery can never provide rear support
- For a base to be able to provide rear support it must be in the same orientation as the base claiming rear support
- A single base can provide rear support to any number of bases in the same grid
- A base in a fortification or in cover will always count as having rear support, overruling the criteria above
- A base in cover counts as rear supported in all cases

Pendraken Miniatures ©2023

Flanks/enfilade

A base that manages to attack an enemy base in the flank has an advantage. This section details situations for claiming a flank:

- A flank can only be claimed as part of a charge
- The defenders in the grid being charged must have their front edge facing at 90 degrees to the charging unit's starting grid
- Flank charge advantage is claimed at the individual base level. These means it might be possible in a single grid to have some bases being able to claim a flank and others that are not
- If target being shot at by enemy where the criteria for a flank, attack are met, excluding any distance restrictions, then it counts as an enfilade shot

The diagram below provides examples of game situations and whether they count as a flank charge or an enfilade shot.

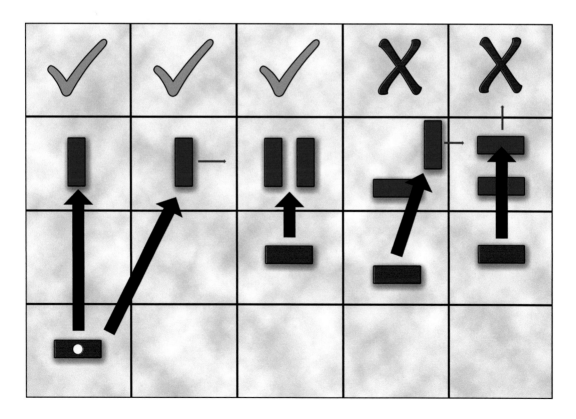

Terrain

This section details the terrain rules. *Muskets & Springfields* defines an individual gird as a terrain piece. The game board is broken down into zones. These are defined below:

Terrain zones

In addition to the sectors the game space is divided into six equal zones for the placement of terrain:

1. These zones are 1/3 width in grids by 1/2 depth in grids of the game space
2. For example, a game on a six-feet-by-four-feet table, each zone will be an area two feet by two feet
3. During the game setup, the campaign theatre the game is set in will dictate the number of zones which will have terrain added
4. Any grid that does not contain terrain is considered as 'good going'

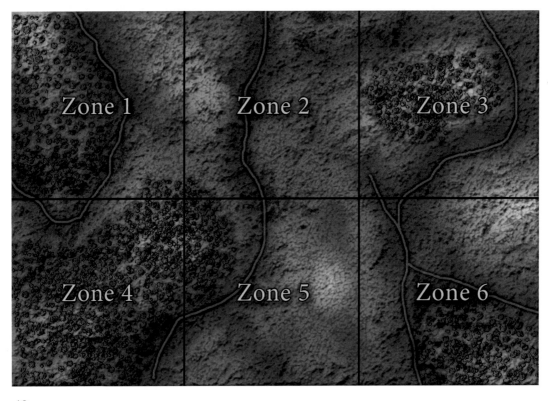

Cover

All terrain except 'good going' provides cover. Cover is further defined as two types – these are non sight-blocking and sight-blocking. Additionally, terrain counts as an obstacle. As there were significant amounts of terrain in the majority of American Civil War battles. Although weapon technology advanced in lethality, their superior ranges were often negated by the presence of woods and undulations on the ground.

Non sight-blocking

A grid with non sight-blocking cover only provides cover to bases inside the grid and bases visible beyond the grid. Non sight-blocking cover can be seen through, except, if a line of sight passes through an additional cover grid of any type, then that grid is classed as sight-blocking. Bases in a Non sight-blocking cover grid or line of sight count as behind cover. Non sight-blocking cover terrain types are detailed in the table below.

Sight-blocking

A grid with sight-blocking cover cannot be seen through. Bases in the grid count as behind cover. A base in any part of a sight-blocking cover grid can be seen but counts as in cover. Sight-blocking terrain types are detailed in the table below. Sight-blocking terrain reduces a base's movement to only one movement action per turn unless the movement is wholly on a road.

Obstacles

These are elements of terrain which provide a defensive quality. To claim the benefit, a base must have their front edge along the edge of the grid and parallel to a table edge. If both players have bases along the same edge, then they both can claim the advantage. Obstacles are detailed in the table below.

Terrain types and effects

The table below details the terrain types, obstacles and if sight-blocking:

Type	Description and game effect	Obstacle	Blocking
Open ground	Majority of area is open. May have a few hedges and fences. Does not provide any form of cover.		
Roads	Marks a significant road. Does not provide any form of cover.		
Rivers/streams	Streams/rivers which are fordable. Impassable to Artillery unless it uses fords or bridges to cross.	X	
Marsh	Marsh and boggy area. Impassable to artillery except via roads.	X	
Major rivers	Impassable rivers. Bridges or fords are required to be able to cross.	X	
Rail roads	Rail track and may be on an embankment. *Players may define the embankment as sight-blocking and/or an obstacle.	X*	X*
Orchards	Ordered rows of trees.		
Woods/forests	Dense woodland with small tracks.	X	X
Fenced fields	Fields with fencing and low crops.	X	
Tall crops	Fields with crops taller than a typical man. A base can be seen.		X
Open fields	Fields without fencing with low crops.		

Type	Description and game effect	Obstacle	Blocking
Farmsteads	Range of dispersed farm buildings with walls and fencing.	X	
Urban areas	Dense housing with streets and gardens.	X	X
Scrub/rocky ground	Area of scrub land and rocky area. Devils Den.	X	
Hills and ridges	Contoured areas. See hills rule below.	X	X

Hills and ridges

Hills and ridges are assumed to be open ground as defined above, unless they have any other terrain placed on them. Hills and ridges have a height level. These are one to three. Level one is the lowest and level three the highest. Ground level is zero.

1. Bases at level one can see over sight-blocking terrain at level zero
2. Level two can see over level zero and one
3. Level three can see over levels zero, one and two

However, if a sight-blocking terrain is placed on a level one then that level becomes a level two for line of sight.

Overhead shooting from higher terrain

Only artillery can shoot overhead of friendly troops if all of the following criteria applies:

1. The artillery is at least one level higher than the friendly base being overshot
2. The artillery can see the target base
3. No friendly bases are to the front of the artillery in the same grid and is the artillery is more than one grid square away from friendly bases on the direct path between the artillery and the target base
4. The target enemy base is less than one grid square from friendly bases on the direct path between the artillery and the target base

Narrative charts

When a Joker or Ace is drawn, both players roll 1D10 and refer to the chart below. If one of these cards is drawn in the first six draws, return to the pack into a random position. The outcomes are applied by the active player first. They are applied army wide. Players cannot use command dice for this roll.

Game setup narrative chart

At the start of the game throw 1D6 and refer to the table below. Also, when the draw pack has only eight cards left roll 1D6 and read off against the table below:

1D6	Narrative	Effect
1	Fog covers the battlefield	Any areas not on a level two hill are in cover for sight and visibility, which is reduced to one unless the base shoots. Lasts for eight draws.
2	Sun is behind the defenders and blinding	Defenders base is in cover for sighting unless base shoots. Lasts for first eight draws. If this was thrown at the start of the game, then counts as a three thrown.
3	Sun is behind the attackers and blinding	Attacker's base is in cover for sighting unless base shoots. Lasts for first eight draws. If this was thrown at the start of the game, then counts as a two thrown.
4–6	'Lovely day for it'	No effect.

Turn narrative chart

1D6	Narrative	Effect
1	Supply issues	Add one attrition hit to all bases with hits.
2	Meal rations found to be mouldy	Add one morale hit to one corps. Owning players choice. Players can not choose a corps to break.
3	Changing weather	Roll against start game narrative generator.
4	Fake rumours spreading	Take one command token from the opponent.
5	'It's steak tonight'	Remove one morale hit from one corps.
6	Replacement supplies	Remove one attrition hit from all bases if >2 hits.

Turns

The rules, after initial setup, use a system of continuous interactive play and not the more common turn system. The current active player is decided by the card drawn from the deck. However, the non-active player will still have the chance to interdict aspects of their opponent's play.

Card deck

A deck of playing cards is used. The face values of the cards (King, Queen, Jack, 10 through to two, the Ace and Joker) each have a distinct impact on the game. The red suits identify the Confederate player as the active player and black suits the Union player.

Ace 100% activation. King (75%), Queen and Jack 50%. 2 through to 10 25%.

Setup

Take a standard deck of playing cards, leaving the jokers in. Shuffle and place to the side of the table face down.

Turn sequence

Start phase

1. Draw one card from the pack and place face up
2. Consult the table below, the exception being the first draw of the pack always counts as the attacker's suit and as an Ace. Battlefield initiative cannot be claimed for this first draw of the game
3. The active player then declares which command formation(s) or the army commander is activated

Actions phase

4. For all active bases, the player declares all actions those bases are going to complete before any dice are rolled
5. A player cannot declare conditional actions
   - An illegal example: Base A will shoot Target Z, if it is not destroyed then Base B will then also shoot otherwise it will advance

- A legal example: Bases A and B will shoot Target Z
- A legal example: Base A will shoot Target Z. Base B will advance to here

6. The expenditure of command tokens is not considered a conditional action, but the use of a command token must be declared prior to any related dice being thrown and the result known

7. Active player completes all declared actions, and the non-active player completes all their responsive actions in the order the active player executes each action

Melee phase

8. Complete all melees for each appropriate grid
9. All melees and outcomes are considered as simultaneous

End of turn phase

10. The active player then removes one attrition hit from all steady bases in the activated commands. No base can have attrition hits removed to less than two remaining for any base with attrition hits

11. The active player may expend one command token per active corps and remove one hit from any base (including nervous ones) in the corps. No base can have attrition hits removed to below two

12. The non-active player may expend one command token in total and remove one hit from any base (including nervous) in one corps. Again, no base can have attrition hits reduced to less than two for any base

13. A player must declare if all their game objectives have been successfully achieved. If so, the game will end at this point and no more cards are drawn

14. When all cards have been drawn from the deck, the game automatically ends at this point

15. Otherwise repeat from 1

Deployment

Unless playing a specific scenario, the following rules are to be applied. Before any deployment starts all bases must be allocated to a corps commander:

Army commander deployment

1. The army commander's base is deployed as the last base to be placed on the board for each army

Deployment zone

1. The deployment zone is the full width of each player's long edge
2. The attacker can deploy <2 grids in depth
3. The defender can deploy <3 grids in depth
4. Large corps can deploy across two adjacent sectors
5. Corps that are not defined as large, must be deployed in a single sector

Deployment sequence

1. When a corps is deployed it must be deployed in full unless it is off table using the Cavalry Raider rule
2. The attacker deploys 75 percent of their corps
3. The defender deploys 50 percent of their corps
4. The attacker deploys their remaining corps and their army commander
5. The defender deploys their remaining corps and their army commander

Game sequence

The following describes the game sequence. The game length clock is managed using a pack of playing cards. A game length is defined by the number of pack-turns. Players agree a length beforehand. One, two or more packs are shuffled before the first card is drawn. The joker cards are left in. These have special effects when drawn. A deck represents the length of time for a single day's daylight.

Game setup phase

This section details the steps for game setup.
1. Roll 1D6 for year (optional) and 1D6 for theatre (optional)
2. Roll 1D6 for attacker/defender. Winner chooses. Re-roll if a draw
3. Place terrain by zones starting with the defender and then alternating
4. Once all terrain zones have been completed each player rolls 1D6 for one objective and picks a second different objective
5. Deployment sequence
6. Allocate command tokens to generals
7. Reveal command token allocation simultaneously
8. Give one order to each corps and keep hidden from the other player
9. Players deploy forces by corps and starting with the attacker
10. Roll 1D6 on start of game narrative table
11. Attacker draws first card. Always counts as an attacker suit. Resolve

12. Draws cards and resolve normally
13. When eight draws are left in the pack. Roll 1D6 on start of game narrative

Turn phase

In the turn phase, players have a continuous sequence of drawing a card to see who the active player is. The rules allow for the non-active player to interrupt. See the turns section above.

Game victory conditions

The game design has the concept of 'sudden death'. The conditions for the game ending are:

- If, after the 25th card has been drawn, a player has achieved all their game objectives, they can claim a win
- After the last card draw and the turn is fully completed
- At any time in the game if the opponent has only one corps left on the board and the opponent has more than one corps on the board, that player can declare victory conditions
- If playing a specific scenario and the objectives have been met. This is a specific condition and is not limited by the 25th card rule in 1 above

Tie breaking

If both players declare victory at the same time, then the following method is to be used to decide a tie:

1. The player with the least number of action points used
   - Cards 2 to 10 = 1
   - J, Q, K = 2
   - A = 3, counting the attackers first draw as an Ace
2. If still a tie, then the player with highest overall morale score wins. Total the morale points inflected for each army.
3. If still a tie, then the winner is the player with highest number of remaining command tokens
4. If there is still a tie, the game is declared a draw

Army builder

The following section provides an army builder to enable players to design forces for a pickup game:

Type	Points per base	Comments
Generals		
Army commander	25	1 per army
Other general	15	One per command group
Upgrade to Exceptional	+5	0–2 total in army
Downgrade to Questionable	−5	
Infantry		
Infantry brigade	20	4–x/Historical formation
Upgrade to with Zouaves	+5	0–1 per corps
Sharpshooters	10	
Cavalry		
Cavalry regiment	10	0-x/Historical formation
Upgrade to cavalry raiders	+5	0–1 per cavalry unit
Artillery		
Artillery (smoothbore)	30	0–2 per corps
Artillery (rifles)	40	Up to one third of total artillery in the army
Irregular forces		
Native American warband	15	0–1 total in army

Note: x = Unlimited, but within limits of allocated corps size.

Example armies

Below are two example armies for a typical pick-up club game. Both are 500 points:

Confederate

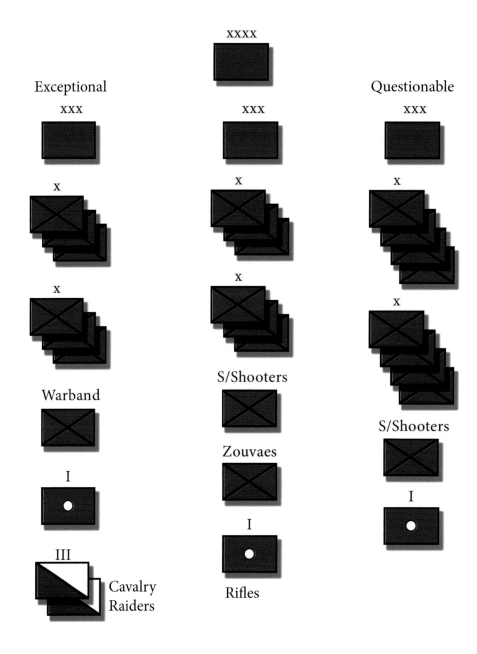

Union

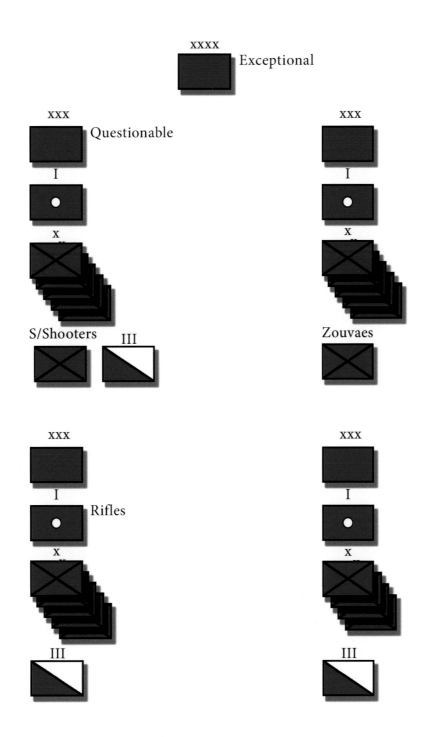

First Battle of Manassas 1861

The First Battle of Manassas, as it is known to the Confederacy, or The First Battle of Bull Run as it was known by the Union. This battle was the first major battle of the war. The Union forces under Brigadier General Irvin McDowell were slow to position themselves for battle. This allowed the Confederates to receive timely reinforcements by rail. A unknown Confederate general, Thomas J. Jackson, led his brigade of Virginians, which stood its ground, earning Jackson his famous nickname 'Stonewall'. After absorbing the initial Union attack the Confederates launched a counterattack, causing the Union to withdraw, which quickly became a rout.

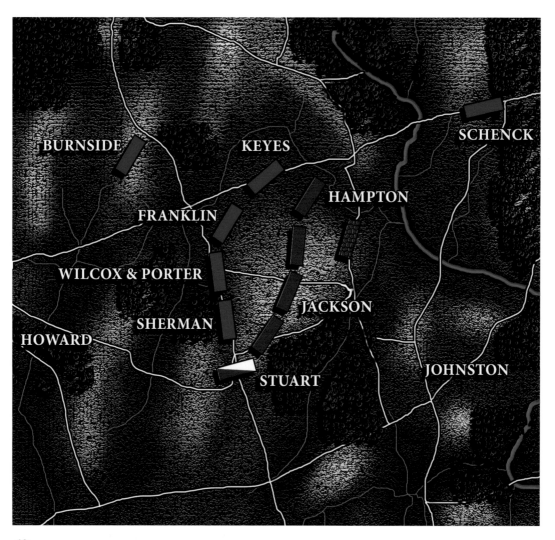

60

Confederate forces

The Army of the Potomac (General Beauregard):

- First Brigade of South Carolinians commanded by Brigadier General Milledge L. Bonham
- Second Brigade commanded by Brigadier General Richard S. Ewell
- Third Brigade commanded by Brigadier General James Longstreet
- Fourth Brigade commanded by Brigadier General David R. Jones
- Fifth Brigade commanded by Colonel Philip Cock
- Sixth Brigade commanded by Colonel Jubal A. Early
- Seventh Brigade commanded by Brigadier General by Colonel Nathan G. Evans
- Reserve Brigade commanded by Colonel Theophilus H. Holmes

The Army of the Shenandoah (General Johnston):

- First Brigade commanded by Colonel Thomas Jackson
- Second Brigade commanded by Colonel Francis S. Bartow
- Third Brigade commanded by Brigade General Barnard E. Bee
- Fourth Brigade commanded by Brigadier General Edmund Kirby Smith
- Cavalry Regiment commanded by Colonel James E. B. Stuart

Union forces

Brigadier General Irvin McDowell

- First Division commanded by Brigadier General Daniel Tyler
    Brigades of Keyes, Sherman and Schenck
- Second Division commanded by Brigadier General David Hunter
    Brigades of Porter and Burnside
- Third Division commanded by Brigadier General Samuel P. Heintzelman
    Brigades of Franklin, Wilcox and Howard
- Fourth Division commanded by Brigadier General Theodore Runyan
    Seven regiments of New Jersey and one regiment of New York volunteer
- Fifth Division commanded by Brigadier General Dixon S. Miles
    Brigades of Blenker and Davies

Battle of Shiloh (first day) 1862

The Battle of Shiloh, also known as Battle of Pittsburgh Landing, was fought across three days. The scenario below focuses on the Confederate attack on day one (6 April 1862). The battle is famous for the church named Shiloh. Johnston's Army of Mississippi attacked Ulysses S. Grant's Army of Tennessee on the first day, in the hope of defeating it, before it could be reinforced by Don Carlos Buell's Army of the Ohio. During the attack Johnston was mortally wounded and although the Confederate attack caught the Union army off guard, it was not able to fully defeat Grant. On the following days, reinforced by Buell, the Union army successfully counter-attacked, reversing the earlier gains of the Confederates. Even though the Union was victorious, they suffered more casualties. Grant was heavily criticised.

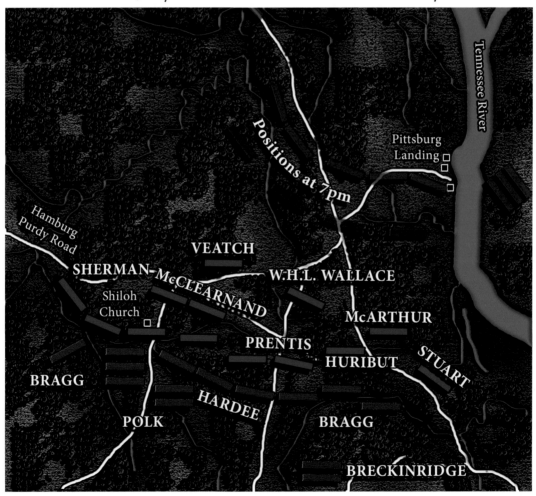

Confederate forces

Army of Mississippi (Albert S. Johnston/Pierre G. T. Beauregard)

- First Army Corps commanded by Leonidas Polk
  4 brigades, 4 artillery batteries and 1 cavalry regiment
- Second Army Corps commanded by Braxton Bragg
  6 brigades, 6 artillery batteries and 1 cavalry regiment
- Third Army Corps commanded by William J. Hardee
  3 brigades, 3 artillery batteries
- Reserve Army Corps commanded by John C. Breckinridge
  3 brigades, 5 artillery batteries and 1 cavalry brigade

Union forces

Army of the Tennessee (Ulysses S. Grant)

- First Division commanded by John A. McClernand
  3 brigades, 3 Artillery batteries and 1 company of cavalry
- Second Division commanded by W. H. L. Wallace
  3 brigades, 4 Artillery batteries and 4 companies of cavalry
- Fourth Division commanded by Stephen A. Hurlbut
  3 brigades, 3 Artillery batteries and 1 company of cavalry
- Fifth Division commanded by William T. Sherman
  4 brigades, 2 Artillery batteries and 1 company of cavalry
- Sixth Division commanded by Benjamin M. Prentiss
  2 brigades, 3 Artillery batteries, 3 regiments and 1 company of cavalry
- To be attached
  6 Artillery batteries and 1 regiment

Army of Ohio (Don Carlos Buell)

Not present on day one of the battle. Arrived in the evening and crossed at Pittsburg Landing ready for the Union counter attack on the 7 April.

Battle of Cedar Mountain 1862

The Battle of Cedar Mountain which also known as Slaughter's Mountain or Cedar Run was fought in the Virginian August heat. This heat hampered Jackson's initial movements of the day. Battle was initiated when Early's Brigade came upon Union cavalry and artillery deployed along the ridge above Cedar Run. After an extended artillery battle the Union forces attacked across fields east of the Culpeper Road. This attack was swift and put strain on the Confederate line, almost breaking it. Confederate artillery deployed on the slope of Cedar Mountain caused casualties in the Union ranks. The attack was in danger of breaking the Confederate line. Jackson steadied the line and the Virginian regiments wheeled and started to enfilade the Union battleline. Eventually the Union forces broke.

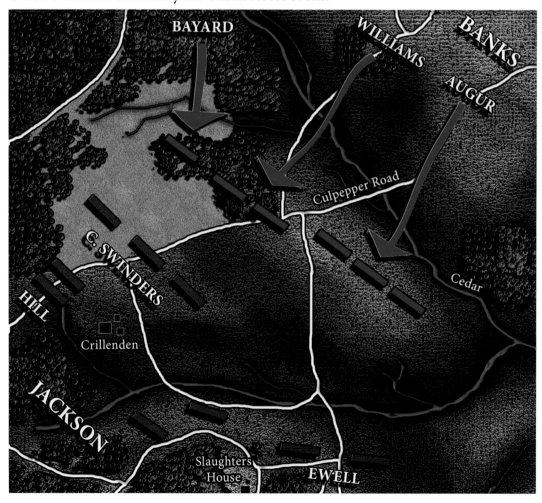

Confederate forces

Left Wing, Army of Northern Virginia (Thomas J. Jackson)

- Ewell's Division commanded by
  3 Brigades and 5 Artillery batteries
- Light Division commanded by A. P. Hill
  7 Brigades and 6 Artillery batteries
- Jackson's Division commanded by Charles S. Winder/William B. Taliaferro
  4 Brigades and 3 Artillery batteries
- Robertson's Cavalry Brigade commanded by Beverly H. Robertson
  4 Cavalry regiments and 1 Artillery battery

Union forces

Second Corps, Army of Virginia (Nathaniel P. Banks)

- First Division commanded by Alpheus S. Williams
  3 Brigades and 3 Artillery batteries
- Second Division commanded by C. C. Augur
  2 Brigades and 1 Artillery battery
- Cavalry Brigade commanded by George D. Bayard
  4 Cavalry regiments

Battle of Gettysburg (Day 1) 1863

The first shot of the Battle of Gettysburg was fired by Lt. Marcellus Jones of the 8th Illinois Cavalry at 7:30 am on 1 July 1863. In the morning, A. P. Hills Confederate corps attacked the Union forces under Reynolds and Doubleday on McPherson's Ridge. By the afternoon Ewell's corps was engaged with Union forces under Howard near Barlow's Knoll to the north of the town of Gettysburg. By the evening the Union forces had been pushed back to Cemetery Hill, to the south of Gettysburg. Hancock was sent by Meade to assume command of the battlefield after Reynolds was killed. Hancock was an extremely capable commander and had Meade's trust.

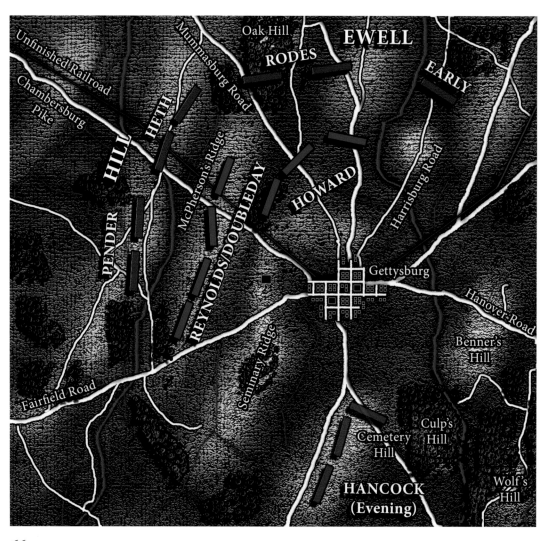

Confederate forces

Army of Northern Virginia (Robert E. Lee)

- Elements of II Corps commanded by Richard S. Ewell
  9 Brigades of Early and Rode's Divisions. 5x Artillery batteries
- Elements of III Corps commanded by A. P. Hill
  4x Brigades of Pender and Heth's Divisions. 5x Artillery batteries

Union forces

Army of the Potomac (George G. Meade)

- Elements of Cavalry Corps, Bulfords I Division (Chambersburg Pike)
  3 Cavalry brigades (7 regiments)
- I Corps commanded by Reynolds and Doubleday
  7 Brigades and 5× Artillery batteries
- II Corps commanded by Winfield S. Hancock
  11 Brigades, 1 Sharpshooters and 6 Artillery batteries
- XI Corps commanded by Oliver O. Howard
  6 Brigades and 5× Artillery batteries

Game notes

This battle can be played using an "in house" random delayed reserves system to allow a steady but slightly uncertainty of when forces will be available. Another alternative is to run the battle as an umpire controlled campaign with changes to remove the element of hindsight for player experience.

Battle of Gettysburg (Day 2) 1863

During the evening of 1 July and the morning of 2 July, the remaining forces arrived on the battlefield. On 2 July, Lee had planned to attack along Meade's line, including having Longstreet attack the southern flank. Lee's intelligence was faulty and to compound the issue, he did not issue orders until 11:00 am. Instead of a coordinated attack along the Union line, Longstreet did not attack until after 4:00 pm. Ewell interpreted his orders as only requiring an artillery bombardment. At 6:00 pm Ewell sent orders to for his infantry to attack. The scenario below focuses on The Peach Orchard attack by McLaws' Division.

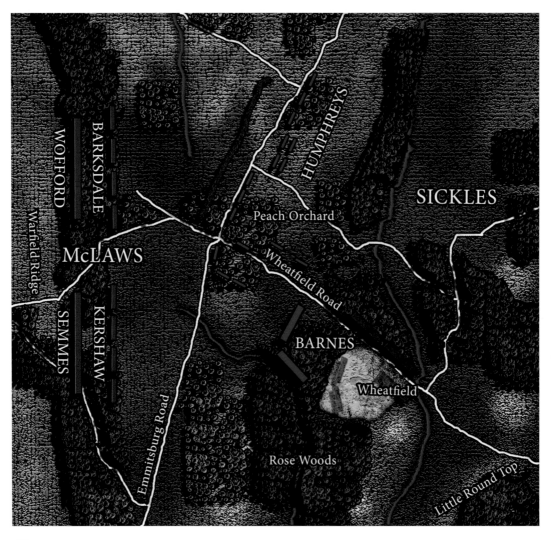

Confederate forces

McLaws' Division (Lafayette McLaws), III Corps (Longstreet)

- Kershaw's Brigade
  6 Regiments
- Barksdale's Brigade
  4 Regiments
- Semmes' Brigade
  4 Regiments
- Wofford's Brigade
  5 Regiments
  2 Sharpshooter bases
- 4 Artillery batteries

Union forces

III Corps (Daniel E. Sickles - Questionable)

- II Division (Andrew A. Humphreys)/1st Brigade
  6 Regiments
- II Division/2nd Brigade
  6 Regiments
- II Division/3rd Brigade
  6 Regiments
- 4 Artillery batteries
- 3 Sharpshooter bases

V Corps (George Sykes)

- I Division (James Barnes)/1st Brigade
  4 Regiments
- I Division/2nd Brigade
  4 Regiments
- I Division/3rd Brigade
  4 Regiments
- 4 Artillery batteries

Battle of Gettysburg (Day 3) 1863

In addition to the infamous Pickett's charge on 3 July, the day also featured the longest artillery bombardment of the war. At around 1:00 pm, 150–170 Confederate guns opened fire to prepare the way for Pickett's attack. Unfortunately, the Confederate artillery was low on ammunition and the bombardment did not significantly affect the Union forces arrayed along Cemetery Ridge. Instead of focusing on Pickett's charge, the scenario below covers Johnson's attack against Slocum's Union forces on Culp's Hill. A "what if" of the battle, is what impact on events of day three if Johnson had broken through and cut the Baltimore Pike and advanced beyond into the rear of Cemetery Ridge?

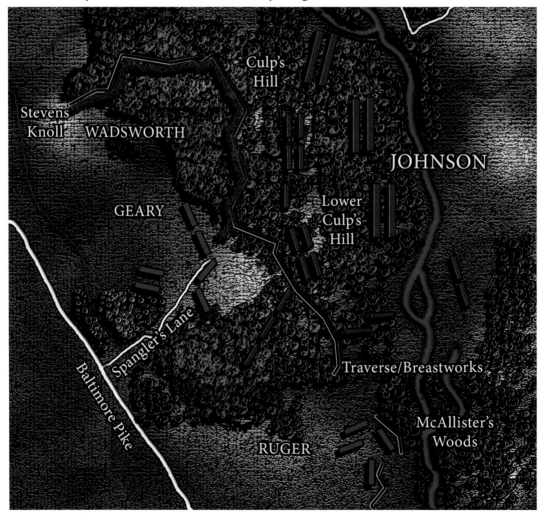

Confederate forces

Johnson's Division (Edward Johnson), II Corps (Richard S. Ewell)

- Jones' Brigade
    2 infantry bases
- Nicholls' Brigade
    3 infantry bases
- Steuart's Brigade
    3 infantry bases
- Stonewall Brigade
    2 infantry bases
- 4 Artillery batteries

Union forces

I Corps

- I Division (Wadsworth)
    2 Brigades
    2 Artillery batteries

XII Corps (Alpheus S. Williams - Game Army Commander)

- I Division (Thomas H. Ruger)
    2 Brigades
- II Division (John W. Geary)
    3 Brigades
- 4 Artillery batteries
- 1 Attached Brigade

Games notes

Traverse/Breastworks count as fortications. All wooded grids are sight-blocking.

10mm American Civil War

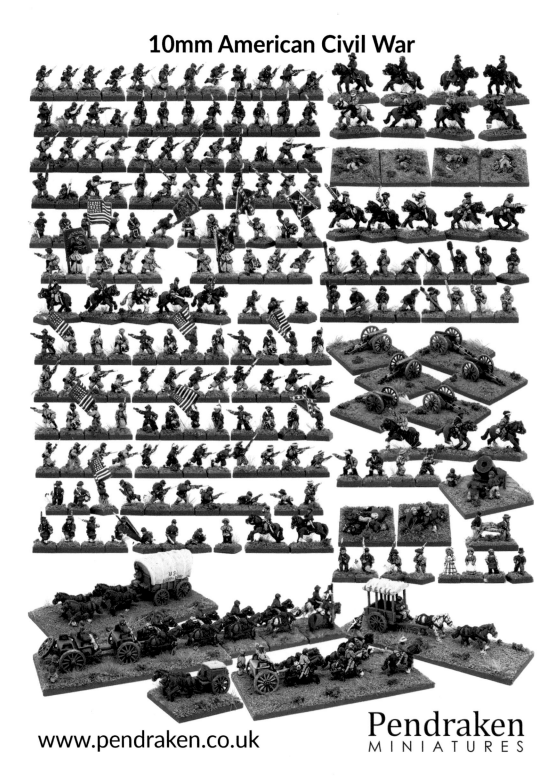

www.pendraken.co.uk

Pendraken
MINIATURES

Quick Reference Sheets

Game setup narrative chart (page 52)

1D6	Narrative	Effect
1	Fog covers the battlefield	Any areas not on a level two hill are in cover for sight and visibility, which is reduced to one unless the base shoots. Lasts for eight draws.
2	Sun is behind the defenders and blinding	Defenders base is in cover for sighting unless base shoots. Lasts for first eight draws. If this was thrown at the start of the game, then counts as a three thrown.
3	Sun is behind the attackers and blinding	Attacker's base is in cover for sighting unless base shoots. Lasts for first eight draws. If this was thrown at the start of the game, then counts as a two thrown.
4–6	'Lovely day for it'	No effect.

Turn narrative chart

1D6	Narrative	Effect
1	Supply issues	Add one attrition hit to all bases with hits.
2	Meal rations found to be mouldy	Add one morale hit to one corps. Owning players choice. Players can not choose a corps to break.
3	Changing weather	Roll against start game narrative generator.
4	Fake rumours spreading	Take one command token from the opponent.
5	'It's steak tonight'	Remove one morale hit from one corps.
6	Replacement supplies	Remove one attrition hit from all bases if >2 hits.

Drawn activation cards

2–10	Jack	Queen	King	Ace	Joker
25% of total Corps/Divs	50% of total Corps/Divs		75% of total Corps/Divs	All Corps/Divs	Narrative Roll and redraw

Game sequence

The following describes the game sequence. The game length clock is managed using a pack of playing cards. A game length is defined by the number of pack-turns. Players agree a length beforehand. One, two or more packs are shuffled before the first card is drawn. The joker cards are left in. These have special effects when drawn. A deck represents the length of time for a single day's daylight.

Game setup phase (page 55)

1. Roll 1D6 for year (optional) and 1D6 for theatre (optional)
2. Roll 1D6 for attacker/defender. Winner chooses. Re-roll if a draw
3. Place terrain by zones starting with the defender and then alternating
4. Once all terrain zones have been completed each player rolls 1D6 for one objective and picks a second different objective
5. Deployment sequence (page XX)
6. Allocate command tokens to generals
7. Reveal command token allocation simultaneously
8. Give one order to each corps and keep hidden from the other player
9. Players deploy forces by corps and starting with the attacker
10. Roll 1D6 on start of game narrative table
11. Attacker draws first card. Always counts as an attacker suit. Resolve

12. Draws cards and resolve normally
13. When eight draws are left in the pack. Roll 1D6 on start of game narrative

Turn phase (page 53)

In the turn phase, players have a continuous sequence of drawing a card to see who the active player is. The rules allow for the non-active player to interrupt. See the turns section above.

Game victory condition

The game design has the concept of 'sudden death'. The conditions for the game ending are:

- If, after the 25th card has been drawn, a player has achieved all their game objectives, they can claim a win
- After the last card draw and the turn is fully completed
- At any time in the game if the opponent has only one corps left on the board and the opponent has more than one corps on the board, that player can declare victory conditions
- If playing a specific scenario and the objectives have been met. This is a specific condition and is not limited by the 25th card rule in 1 above
- Tie breaking (page XX)

Turns (page 53)

The rules, after initial setup, use a system of continuous interactive play and not the more common turn system. The current active player is decided by the card drawn from the deck. However, the non-active player will still have the chance to interdict aspects of their opponent's play.

Card deck

A deck of playing cards is used. The face values of the cards (King, Queen, Jack, 10 through to two, the Ace and Joker) each have a distinct impact on the game. The red suits identify the Confederate player as the active player and black suits the Union player.

Setup

Take a standard deck of playing cards, leaving the jokers in. Shuffle and place to the side of the table face down.

Turn sequence

Start phase

1. Draw one card from the pack and place face up
2. Consult the table below, the exception being the first draw of the pack always counts as the attacker's suit and as an Ace.

3. Battlefield initiative cannot be claimed for this first draw of the game
4. The active player then declares which command formation(s) or the army commander is activated

Actions phase (page 33)

5. For all active bases, the player declares all actions those bases are going to complete before any dice are rolled
6. A player cannot declare conditional actions
   - An illegal example: Base A will shoot Target Z, if it is not destroyed then Base B will then also shoot otherwise it will advance
   - A legal example: Bases A and B will shoot Target Z
   - A legal example: Base A will shoot Target Z. Base B will advance to here
7. The expenditure of command tokens is not considered a conditional action, but the use of a command token must be declared prior to any related dice being thrown and the result known
8. Active player completes all declared actions, and the non-active player completes all their responsive actions in the order the active player executes each action

Melee phase

9. Complete all melees for each appropriate grid
10. All melees and outcomes are considered as simultaneous

End of turn phase

11. The active player then removes one attrition hit from all steady bases in the activated commands. No base can have attrition hits removed to less than two remaining for any base with attrition hits
12. The active player may expend one command token per active corps and remove one hit from any base (including nervous ones) in the corps. No base can have attrition hits removed to below two
13. The non-active player may expend one command token in total and remove one hit from any base (including nervous) in one corps. Again, no base can have attrition hits reduced to less than two for any base
14. A player must declare if all their game objectives have been successfully achieved. If so, the game will end at this point and no more cards are drawn
15. When all cards have been drawn from the deck, the game automatically ends at this point
16. Otherwise repeat from 1

Melee (page 43)

Situation	Adjust
Base	5
Zouaves and Native American warbands	−2
Steady vs nervous	−1
Fighting enemy in cover/obstacle	+1
Or, fighting enemy in fortifications	+2
Mounted cavalry vs infantry base	Re-roll hits
First round charging into a flank	Re-roll misses

Base type	Dice
Infantry base	6D10
Cavalry (dismounted) or Zouaves	4D10
Native Indian war party in cover	4D10
Native Indian war party not in cover	2D10
Cavalry (mounted)	
Artillery crew	2D10
Sharpshooters	1D10
For each two attrition hits	−1D10
A base will always get to throw 1D10.	

For outcomes see page 44.

Army commander actions (page 25)

Cost	Action
One token	Reform one corps attrition if not the active player.
	Force a success on 1D10.
	Add 1D10 to any throw that requires D10s.
	Change any corps orders if the active player.
Free	Move once per turn as mounted cavalry if the active player.
	If present in the same grid allow 1D10 to be re-rolled per throw for any base in the army, that has not been re-rolled.
	Grabbing battlefield initiative

Other generals actions (page 25)

Cost	Action (see command actions section)
Free	Move once per turn as mounted cavalry when part of an activated corps.
	If present in the same grid allow 1D10 to be re-rolled per throw for a base in their command, that has not been re-rolled.

Charge and movement (page 36)

Base	Distance
Any moving through any sight-blocking cover (expect sharpshooters) Total movement allowed in the current turn. Ignore if fully on road during the turn	1
Infantry base	
Dismounted cavalry	
Charge distance (all)	
Shoot and scoot	
Sharpshooters	2
Mounted cavalry	
Limbered artillery	
Scoot only	
Movement entirely on road	+1 to above

Morale Tests (page 28)

During the game there will be situations that will require a morale test to be taken. The situations are defined below:

1. After receiving attrition hits in a single turn and the base has greater than two attrition hits applied

2. Check to charge or receive a charge. A morale check resulting in a failure to charge does not inflict a morale hit on the testing base's corps

Situation by base	Adjust
If Zouaves or a Native American war party testing to charge or be charged	Auto pass
Base	5
Has other steady bases in same grid	−1
If counting rear supported	
For a general in line of command (maximum of one) in the same grid	
For each attrition hit over two	+1
If charging from cover into the open/from open into cover	
If the required score is more than 10, then it is an automatic failure by one, and command tokens cannot be applied to affect this result.	

Outcomes

After throwing the D10, note the difference thrown against the required score. Consult the table below:

Effect (Not chargers)	Result
Pass, remove one morale hit from the unit's corps	Natural 10
Pass, continue	equal/greater than 0
Fail, base is immediately destroyed	Less than 0
Effect (Chargers)	**Result**
Fail, does not charge and no other effect is applied	<0

Shooting (page 36)

Small arms	Range in grids	Artillery	Range in grids
All small arms	1	Smoothbore	5
If skirmishers are deployed	2	Rifled	6
Any sharpshooters			

Condition	Adjustment
Base factor for all shooting	5
All	
If shooting and scooting	+1
Target is sharpshooters or deployed artillery	
Shooters (small arms)	
If target in cover	+1
Has >1 hits currently applied	
If sharpshooters and range to target is 1	−1
If sharpshooters shooting at artillery	
Has not or will not move this turn	
Steady shooting at *nervous*	
Shooters (smoothbore artillery)	
Target range is >1	+2
Target range is 1	−1
Shooters (rifled artillery)	
Target range is >1	+1
Rifled artillery shooting at artillery >1	−1

Shooting dice

The number of shooting dice per base is defined in the following table:

Small arms	Dice
Infantry base	4D10
Infantry base with skirmishers deployed	3D10
Dismounted cavalry base	3D10
Dismounted cavalry base with skirmishers deployed	2D10
If target is enfiladed and target not sharpshooters	Auto 1 hit + dice thrown result(s)
If target is in fortifications	Re-roll hits
Sharpshooters	**Dice**
Sharpshooters (all situations)	1D10
Artillery	**Dice**
Target at range of one (smoothbore)	5D10
Target at range of one (rifled)	4D10
Target at range of over one	2D10
Target at range of six	1D10
If target is enfiladed and target not sharpshooters	Auto 1 hit + dice thrown result(s)

Outcomes

Consult the table below and resolve any effects:

Effect	Outcome
Each success per D10 (Except a natural 10)	One attrition hit
Small arms at range one throwing a natural 10. Suppressing fire	Two attrition hits
Artillery only shooting at more than one grid: (bounce through). On a natural 1D10, for each base except skirmisher markers, sharpshooters or a general	Throw 1D10 per unit usiShortlyng same value and apply as above
Hits applied and if target base has more than two attrition hits	Morale test